SMALL GROUP SERIES

Smart Choices

Making Your Way through Life

Harold Eppley
Rochelle Melander

Augsburg Fortress, Minneapolis

Contents

Introduction 3
Series introduction 5
1 Choices, Messages, and Principles 11
2 Considering Your Own Principles 19
3 From Principles to Mission Statement 26
4 Creating Your Own Mission Statement 32
5 Christian Principles into Practice 39
6 Smart Choices for a Lifetime 45
Appendix 52
    Group directory 52
    Group commitments 53
    Prayer requests 53
    Prayers 54
    Resources 54
    Response form 55

INTERSECTIONS
Small Group Series

Smart Choices
Making Your Way through Life

Developed in cooperation with the Division for Congregational Ministries

George S. Johnson, series introduction
Catherine Malotky and Jill Carroll Lafferty, editors
The Wells Group, series design
Cover photo: Digital Stock copyright © 1998
Illustrator: Brian Jensen

Materials identified as *LBW* are from *Lutheran Book of Worship*, copyright 1978.

Scripture quotations are from New Revised Standard Version Bible, copyright 1989 Division of Christian Education of the National Council of the Churches of Christ in the United States of America. Used by permission.

Copyright © 1998 Augsburg Fortress
All rights reserved. May not be reproduced.
ISBN 0-8066-3722-6
Manufactured in U.S.A.

  2 3 4 5 6 7 8 9 0 1 2 3 4 5 6 7 8 9

Introduction

Seeking smart choices

Paper or plastic? Fast food or health food? Rent or buy? Savings accounts or mutual funds? Regardless of our age or life situation, each day we face many choices, both small and large. As Christians we may hope that our daily decisions are influenced by our faith. Yet, for all of us, making wise decisions is difficult.

Janet, a single mother, struggles for balance as she juggles a full-time job, housework, and parenting her two children. Bob seeks to make the most of his retirement after working for 40 years. Diane, a lawyer in her 40s, recently has begun to reevaluate her priorities and is considering a career change. Though their life circumstances vary, these three people share a common dilemma—how to put their Christian principles into practice in their daily lives.

No doubt, like Janet, Bob, and Diane, you too have struggled to juggle responsibilities, set priorities, and make smart choices. Most of us are confronted by a variety of messages, both subtle and urgent, about how to live. These often conflicting messages can leave us feeling confused about which choices will be most helpful to us. As Christians, our challenge is to sift through all of these messages and choose a life that is consistent with our principles.

The purpose of this study

This small group study provides an opportunity for you to gather with other Christians who are seriously seeking to put their principles into practice. In this study you will:

- discuss the variety of messages that influence the choices you make every day.
- review the choices you make and consider what these choices reveal about the principles you value.
- explore your own unique gifts and talents.
- create a personal mission statement based on your principles and gifts.
- consider how your mission statement impacts your relationships and roles.
- identify resources that can provide support as you seek to put your Christian principles into practice.

The blessing of community

The intent of this study is to help you focus your life choices around what you most value. Of course, you could buy a self-help book and do this on your own, but by reflecting on your individual choices and values within a small group you will receive the blessing of community. The stories and experiences of others can teach you about your own spiritual journey. You will also have the added benefit of knowing that others are supporting and encouraging you as you make positive changes in your life.

Individual reflection time

To fully benefit from your participation in this group you will need to take time between sessions for individual reflection. Your independent work will include considering which principles you value most, writing a mission statement, and seeking out the support of family and friends. It might be helpful to set aside a journal or notebook for your work in this study.

A final note

This study is packed full of information, questions, and exercises designed to help you consider how you make choices in your life. Each chapter theme builds on work done on the previous theme. For this reason, your group will benefit from proceeding slowly and carefully through each section, taking time to do all the exercises, and answering each question. If your time together is relatively short (an hour or less), you may consider dividing each chapter theme into two sessions.

Welcome to *Smart Choices*. May your participation in this group give you the insight and encouragement to make smart choices for a lifetime.

Introducing the series

Intersections
SMALL GROUP SERIES

Welcome into the family of those who are part of small groups! *Intersections Small Group Series* **will help you and other members of your group build relationships and discover ways to connect the Christian faith with your everyday life.**

This book is prepared for those who want to make a difference in this world, who want to grow in their Christian faith, as well as for those who are beginning to explore the Christian faith. The information in this introduction to the *Intersections* **small group experience can help your group make the most out of your time together.**

Biblical encouragement

"Do not be conformed to this world, but be transformed by the renewing of your minds, so that you may discern what is the will of God—what is good and acceptable and perfect" (Romans 12:2).

Small groups provide an atmosphere where the Holy Spirit can transform lives. As you share your life stories and learn together, God's Spirit can work to enlighten and direct you.

Strength is provided to face the pressures to conform to forces and influences that are opposed to what is "good and acceptable and perfect." To "be transformed" is an ongoing experience of God's grace as we take up the cross and follow Jesus. Changed lives happen as we live in community with one another. Small groups encourage such change and growth.

What is a small group?

A number of definitions and descriptions of the small group ministry experience exist throughout the church. Roberta Hestenes, a Presbyterian pastor and author, defines a small group as an intentional face-to-face gathering of three to 12 people who meet regularly with the common purpose of discovering and growing in the possibilities of the abundant life.

Whatever definition you use, the following characteristics are important.

Small—Seven to 10 people is ideal so that everyone can be heard and no one's voice is lost. More than 12 members makes genuine caring difficult.

Intentional—Commitment to the group is a high priority.

Personal—Sharing experiences and insights is more important than mastering content.

Conversational—Leaders that facilitate conversation, rather than teach, are the key to encouraging participation.

Friendly—Having a warm, accepting, nonjudgmental atmosphere is essential.

Christ-centered—The small group experience is biblically based, related to the real world, and founded on Christ.

Features of Intersections Small Group Series

A small group model

A number of small group ministry models exist. Most models include three types of small groups:

- *Discipleship groups*—where people gather to grow in Christian faith and life.

- *Support and recovery groups*—which focus on special interests, concerns, or needs.

- *Ministry groups*—which have a task-oriented focus.

Intersections Small Group Series presently offers material for discipleship groups and support and recovery groups.

For discipleship groups, this series offers a variety of courses with Bible study at the center. What makes a discipleship group different from traditional group Bible studies? In discipleship groups, members bring their life experience to the exploration of the biblical material.

For support and recovery groups, *Intersections Small Group Series* offers topical material to assist group members in dealing with issues related to their common experience, hurt, or interest.

Ministry groups can benefit from an environment that includes prayer, biblical reflection, and relationship building, in addition to their task focus.

Four essentials

Prayer, personal sharing, biblical reflection, and a group ministry task are part of each time you gather. These are all important for Christian community to be experienced. Each of the six chapter themes in each book includes:

- short prayers to open and close your time together.

- carefully worded questions to make personal sharing safe, nonthreatening, and voluntary.

- a biblical base from which to understand and discover the power and grace of God. God's Word is the compass that keeps the group on course.

- a group ministry task to encourage both individuals and the group as a whole to find ways to put faith into action.

Flexibility

Each book contains six chapter themes that may be covered in six sessions or easily extended for groups that meet for a longer period of time. Each chapter theme is organized around two to three main topics with supplemental material to make it easily adaptable to your small group's needs. You need not use all the material. Most themes will work well for 1½- to 2-hour sessions, but a variety of scheduling options is possible.

Bible based

Each of the six chapter themes in the book includes one or more Bible texts printed in its entirety from the New Revised Standard Version of the Bible. This makes it easy for all group members to read and learn from the same text. Participants will be encouraged through questions, with exercises, and by other group members to address biblical texts in the context of their own lives.

User friendly

The material is prepared in such a way that it is easy to follow, practical, and does not require a professional to lead it. Designating one to be the facilitator to guide the group is important, but there is no requirement for this person to be theologically trained or an expert in the course topic. Many times options are given so that no one will feel forced into any set way of responding.

Group goals and process

1. Creating a group covenant or contract for your time together will be important. During your first meeting, discuss these important characteristics of all small groups and decide how your group will handle them.

Confidentiality—Agreeing that sensitive issues that are shared remain in the group.

Regular attendance—Agreeing to make meetings a top priority.

Nonjudgmental behavior—Agreeing to confess one's own shortcomings, if appropriate, not those of others, and not giving advice unless asked for it.

Prayer and support—Being sensitive to one another, listening, becoming a caring community.

Accountability—Being responsible to each other and open to change.

Items in your covenant should be agreed upon by all members. Add to the group covenant as you go along. Space to record key aspects is included in the back of this book. See page 53.

2. Everyone is responsible for the success of the group, but do arrange to have one facilitator who can guide the group process each time you meet.

The facilitator is not a teacher or healer. Teaching, learning, and healing happen from the group experience. The facilitator is more of a shepherd who leads the flock to where they can feed and drink and feel safe.

Remember, an important goal is to experience genuine love and community in a Christ-centered atmosphere. To help make this happen, the facilitator encourages active listening and honest sharing. This person allows the material to facilitate opportunities for self-awareness and interaction with others.

Leadership is shared in a healthy group, but the facilitator is the one designated to set the pace, keep the group focused, and enable the members to support and care for each other.

People need to sense trust and freedom as the group develops; therefore, avoid "shoulds" or "musts" in your group.

3. Taking on a group ministry task can help members of your group balance personal growth with service to others.

In your first session, identify ways your group can offer help to others within the congregation or in your surrounding community. Take time at each meeting to do or arrange for that ministry task. Many times it is in the doing that we discover what we believe or how God is working in our lives.

4. Starting or continuing a personal action plan offers a way to address personal needs that you become aware of in your small group experience.

For example, you might want to spend more time in conversation with a friend or spouse. Your action plan might state, "I plan to visit with Terry two times before our next small group meeting."

If you decide to pursue a personal action plan, consider sharing it with your small group. Your group can be helpful in at least three ways: by giving support; helping to define the plan in realistic, measurable ways; and offering a source to whom you can be accountable.

5. Prayer is part of small group fellowship. There is great power in group prayer, but not everyone feels free to offer spontaneous prayer. That's okay.

Learning to pray aloud takes time and practice. If you feel uncomfortable, start with simple and short prayers. And remember to pray for other members between sessions.

Use page 53 in the back of this book to note prayer requests made by group members.

6. Consider using a journal to help reflect on your experiences and insights between meeting times.

Writing about feelings, ideas, and questions can be one way to express yourself; plus it helps you remember what so often gets lost with time.

The "Daily Walk" component includes material that can get your journaling started. This, of course, is up to you and need not be done on any regular schedule. Even doing it once a week can be time well spent.

How to use this book

The material provided for each chapter theme is organized around some key components. If you are the facilitator for your small group, be sure to read this section carefully.

The facilitator's role is to establish a hospitable atmosphere and set a tone that encourages participants to share, reflect, and listen to each other. Some important practical things can help make this happen.

- Whenever possible meet in homes. Be sure to provide clear directions about how to get there.
- Use name tags for several sessions.
- Place the chairs in a circle and close enough for everyone to hear and feel connected.
- Be sure everyone has access to a book; preparation will pay off.

Welcoming

In this study, group members will reflect on their personal choices and principles. The sessions are intended to provide a sort of retreat from the demands of daily life. During the sessions, participants can consider how to make smarter choices.

Provide a meeting space that both allows for privacy and creates a retreat atmosphere. A comfortable room in the church or a participant's home would work well. Try to minimize distractions by closing doors, turning off the telephone ringer, and playing soft instrumental music.

Welcome group members personally as they arrive. Provide name tags for each session—they put everyone on equal footing and will help newcomers to feel at home.

Focus

Each of the six chapter themes in this book has a brief focus statement. Read it aloud. It will give everyone a sense of the direction for each session and provide some boundaries so that people will not feel lost or frustrated trying to cover everything. The focus also connects the theme to the course topic.

Community building

This opening activity is crucial to a relaxed, friendly atmosphere. It will prepare the ground for gradual group development. Two "Community Building" options are provided under each theme. With the facilitator giving his or her response to the questions first, others are free to follow.

One purpose for this section is to allow everyone to participate as he or she responds to nonthreatening questions. The activity serves as a check-in time when participants are invited to share how things are going or what is new.

Make this time light and fun; remember, humor is a welcome gift. Use 15 to 20 minutes for this activity in your first few sessions and keep the entire group together.

During your first meeting, encourage group members to write down names and phone numbers (when appropriate) of the other members, so people can keep in touch. Use page 52 for this purpose.

Discovery

This component focuses on exploring the theme for your time together, using material that is read, and questions and exercises that encourage sharing of personal insights and experiences.

Reading material includes a Bible text with supplemental passages and commentary written by the topic writer. Have volunteers read the Bible texts aloud. Read the commentary aloud only when it seems helpful. The main passage to be used is printed so that everyone operates from a common translation and sees the text.

"A Further Look" is included in some places to give you additional study material if time permits. Use it to explore related passages and questions. Be sure to have your own Bible handy.

Questions and exercises related to the theme will invite personal sharing and storytelling. Keep in mind that as you listen to each other's stories, you are inspired to live more fully in the grace and will of God. Such exchanges make Christianity relevant and transformation more likely to happen. Caring relationships are key to clarifying one's beliefs. Sharing personal experiences and insights is what makes the small group spiritually satisfying.

Most people are open to sharing their life stories, especially if they're given permission to do so and they know someone will actively listen. Starting with the facilitator's response usually works best. On some occasions you may want to break the group into units of three or four persons to explore certain questions. When you reconvene, relate your experience to the whole group.

Wrap-up

Plan your schedule so that there will be enough time for wrapping up. This time can include work on your group ministry task, review of key discoveries during your time together, identifying personal and prayer concerns, closing prayers, and the Lord's Prayer.

The facilitator can help the group identify and plan its ministry task. Introduce the idea and decide on your group ministry task during "Wrap-up" time in the first session. Tasks need not be grandiose. Activities might include:

- ministry in your community, such as "adopting" a food shelf, clothes closet, or homeless shelter; sponsoring equipment, food, or clothing drives; or sending members to staff the shelter.

- ministry to members of the congregation, such as writing notes to those who are ill or bereaved.

- congregational tasks where volunteers are always needed, such as serving refreshments during the fellowship time after worship, stuffing envelopes for a church mailing, or taking responsibility for altar preparations for one month.

Depending upon the task, you can use part of each meeting time to carry out or plan the task.

In the "Wrap-up," allow time for people to share insights and encouragements and to voice special prayer requests. Just to mention someone who needs prayer is a form of prayer. The "Wrap-up" time may include a brief worship experience with candles, prayers, and singing. You might form a circle and hold hands. Silence can be effective. If you use the Lord's Prayer in your group, select the version that is known in your setting. There is space on page 54 to record the version your group uses. Another closing prayer is also printed on page 54. Before you go, ask members to pray for one another during the week. Remember also any special concerns or prayer requests.

Daily walk

Seven Bible readings and a verse, thought, and prayer for the journey related to the material just discussed are provided for those who want to keep the theme before them between sessions. These brief readings may be used for devotional time. Some group members may want to memorize selected passages. The Bible readings can also be used for supplemental study by the group if needed. Prayer for other group members can also be part of this time of personal reflection.

A word of encouragement

No material is ever complete or perfect for every situation or group. Creativity and imagination will be important gifts for the facilitator to bring to each theme. Keep in mind that it is in community that we are challenged to grow in Jesus Christ. Together we become what we could not become alone. It is God's plan that it be so.

For additional resources and ideas see *Starting Small Groups—and Keeping Them Going* (Minneapolis: Augsburg Fortress, 1995).

1 Choices, Messages, and Principles

Focus

As Christians, we believe there are fundamental principles that can serve as a foundation for the way we live and affect the choices we make.

Community building

- Share your name and tell why this group interested you.
- On your day off, would you be more likely to:
  a. get up early or sleep as late as possible?
  b. plan the day from start to finish or just let it happen?
  c. eat a big breakfast or nothing at all?
  d. take a walk or go shopping?
  e. spend time with friends or read a favorite book?
  f. listen to classical music or rock and roll?
  g. attend to a household chore you've been neglecting or take a nap?
  h. munch on potato chips or dig into a bowl of ice cream?

Encourage group members to respond to each of the items with a show of hands. Add "neither" as a response to each item and allow group members to contribute additional suggestions. There are no right or wrong answers.

Option

On paper, list some of the choices you have made in the last 24 hours. It can include relatively trivial choices like eating toast for breakfast instead of cereal. After several minutes share your choices and talk about which were easy or difficult to make, which didn't even seem like choices, and which you might make again.

Opening prayer

Guiding God, when we are overwhelmed by the many messages we hear, teach us how to listen for your voice. Speak to us as we study your Word and contemplate our lives. Amen

Discovery

Read aloud and discuss.

Choices and messages

We make an enormous number of choices every day. Our decisions range from relatively insignificant choices—like what color socks we will wear—to more weighty decisions, such as where we work. All of these choices, large and small, are influenced by a variety of factors—our principles, our relationships, and the various messages we hear each day. Some of the sources of these messages include:

    a. the media (magazines, television, newspapers, Internet)
    b. books
    c. parents
    d. children
    e. friends
    f. school
    g. various "sub-cultures" in which we live and work (occupational, regional, racial, economic, religious, gender, other.)

You might hear the message from a local community group that "responsible citizens recycle." At work you might hear the message that "in order to succeed in your occupation you need to work 70 hours a week." These messages may affect the daily choices you make.

Discuss other examples of messages you receive from each of the sources.

- Which of these sources of messages do you think are the most influential in our society today?
- Share some of the messages that are the most powerful to you.
- Which of these messages do you find helpful? Which are unhelpful?

Discuss.

Consider this

> How might the messages in this picture affect your choice of:
> a. what you eat for dinner?
> b. how you spend your money?
> c. what you do with your time?
> d. how you treat others?

Read aloud.

The relationship factor

Although we receive messages from many sources, we do not place equal value on all of the messages we hear. We tend to place more importance on the opinions of those we love and respect than on the ideas of those we do not know well. The people we value the most have the greatest influence on the choices we make.

Read and discuss as a group.

Madeleine's story

Madeleine, a high school junior and an honor student, is trying to decide what to do after high school graduation. She has asked several people for advice. Madeleine confesses to being confused, saying, "I really want to do the right thing—but sometimes it is difficult to know what the right thing is!" Here is some of the advice Madeleine has heard:

Her mother says: "Whatever you choose is fine with me—just don't move too far away from home."

Her father says: "Do something that will make me proud of you. Train for a career in which you can make lots of money."

Her friend Cindy says: "You have the rest of your life to worry about working. Take some time off and party!"

Her boss says: "Stay here and work. In a few years you could be a manager like me."

- Considering the advice Madeleine's friends and family gave to her, what do you imagine each of them values most?
- If you were Madeleine's counselor, what advice would you give her?
- Consider some of the relationships that are important in your own life. How do these relationships influence the choices you make?

A further look

Divide into three groups, each looking up one of the scripture passages. Read the passage and discuss the questions. Share the story and your insights with the larger group.

Look up the following passages:
    Matthew 1:18-25
    Mark 1:16-20
    Luke 8:40, 42b-48.

- What choices are being made?
- What do you imagine are some of the factors that influenced these choices?

Discovery

Read aloud and discuss.

Christian principles

The *American Heritage Dictionary of the English Language* defines "principle" as "a basic truth, law, or assumption." Stephen R. Covey, in his book *The Seven Habits of Highly Effective People*, writes: "Principles are guidelines for human conduct that are proven to have enduring, permanent value."[1] Covey suggests these principles as examples: integrity, honesty, human dignity, service, and patience.

Principles serve as a foundation for the way we live our lives and affect the choices we make. All religions are based on principles. As Christians, we share some principles with people of other faiths. In this study, while we will consider many "universal" principles, we will focus on the principles that are central to the Christian faith.

1. From *The Seven Habits of Highly Effective People*, 35.

The ultimate purpose of seeking to live by Christian principles is to strengthen our relationship with God. In addition, structuring our lives around central principles will enable us to make wiser choices—resulting in healthier relationships and schedules. If we live by the principles God has set before us, our lives will be richer. God knows what is good for us!

Jesus' teachings and example provide a helpful framework for understanding Christian principles. For example, one principle that might guide a Christian's life is forgiveness (see Matthew 18:21-22). A search of Scripture reveals other principles. The Ten Commandments identify a number of principles including commitment (Exodus 20:14) and respect (Exodus 20:12).

You may want to post principles on newsprint.

- As a group, make a list of principles that you think are central to the Christian faith. (If you are having difficulty, here is a list to get you started: justice, mercy, hospitality, trust in God, gratitude)

Discuss as a group.

Consider this

What do each of these comments say about making choices? How would you respond to each of these people?

- George: "Eat, drink, and be merry—for tomorrow we die."
- Ken: "My success depends on nobody but me. I am the only one who can make a difference in my life."
- Lin: "I do my best to make good choices. The rest of life, I entrust to God."
- Jan: "I'm trying to do the right thing and I am overwhelmed. How do I balance the needs of my children, my spouse, my church, and God's creation? It seems to be an impossible task!"

A further look

Read and discuss.

- What are the challenges that keep us from choosing wisely? The writer of Ephesians said, "We must no longer be children, tossed to and fro and blown about by every wind of doctrine, by people's trickery, by their craftiness in deceitful scheming" (4:14).

- Why do you think most people have trouble living by Christian principles?
    a. It's too hard.
    b. Their friends will mock them.
    c. They have no time.
    d. They don't want to.
    e. Other.
- What do you think are some of the things that toss you to and fro and keep you from choosing well?

Discovery

Read and discuss.

Consider this

"We can choose how we live. God created us with the power to choose. Perhaps that is part of what it means to be created in God's image. By choosing well, we can make our lives more manageable and more meaningful."

From 'Tis a Gift to Be Simple, 11

Give an example of how you think choosing well could make your life either more manageable or more meaningful.

Ask group members to discuss these issues. Invite group members to record their ideas on the "Group commitments" page in the appendix.

Group goals

- What are your goals for the study of this topic? Use the list below or create your own. Try to agree on two or three group goals.
    a. Meet new people.
    b. Learn how to make better choices.
    c. Understand God's purpose for my life.
    d. Study God's Word.
    e. Grow closer to God.
    f. Support other members of the group through prayer and dialogue.
    g. Examine how we live our lives.
    h. Learn about Christian principles.
    i. Other.

Group commitments

■ What commitments will you make to one another? Use the categories listed as a guide for setting ground rules for your group. See the series introduction (page 5) for more information.
    a. confidentiality
    b. regular attendance
    c. nonjudgmental behavior
    d. prayer
    e. support (during and between sessions)
    f. accountability

Group ministry task

Consider together how you as a group can help others in your church and community. Look at pages 7 and 53 of this book and *Starting Small Groups—and Keeping Them Going*, Training Handout 20A, for suggestions.

Wrap-up

See page 10 in the introduction for a description of "Wrap-up."

Before you go, take time for the following:

- Group ministry task

- Review

See page 54 for suggested closing prayers. Page 53 can be used for listing ongoing prayer requests.

- Personal concerns and prayer concerns

- Closing prayers

Daily walk

Bible readings

Day 1
Jeremiah 17:7-8

Day 2
Matthew 7:24-27

Day 3
Mark 4:3-9, 13-20

Day 4
Romans 12:1-2

Day 5
2 Corinthians 5:17-20

Day 6
Psalm 127:1-2

Day 7
Colossians 3:12-17

Verse for the journey

"I am about to do a new thing; now it springs forth, do you not perceive it? I will make a way in the wilderness and rivers in the desert" (Isaiah 43:19).

Thought for the journey

Picture your "ideal" life. How is it similar or different from your current life? (Be prepared to share some of your reflections at the next meeting.)

Prayer for the journey

Ever-present God, in all our choices—small and large—remind us to be faithful to you. Amen

2 Considering Your Own Principles

Focus

Examining the choices you make provides insight into the principles by which you live.

Community building

You may want to play meditative music softly.

Option

Tell a story about a memorable birthday celebration (it may be, but does not have to be, your own). What made it meaningful?

- Remember a meaningful event in your life. Close your eyes. Try to recall some of the sights, smells, and sounds of that experience. Who was present? What happened?

  After four to five minutes have passed, take a moment to stretch and then come together as a group. If you wish, share with the group the experience you remembered.

Check-in

- Share a high point and a low point from your week. When all have shared, pray for the person on your right, saying: "Emmanuel, God with us, bless (*name*) in his/her journey through life."

Opening prayer

God of all times and places, give us the courage and insight to examine our own lives with honesty. In the discoveries we make enable us to see your enduring presence. Amen

Discovery

Group reporting

Share with the group one or two aspects of your "ideal" life (see chapter 1, "Thought for the Journey").

Read aloud and discuss.

Mentors on the journey

Sometimes the best way to consider how to live our own lives is to look to the example of others. Family members, friends, teachers, and coworkers can be our mentors as we seek to make smart choices.

Think about someone you admire because of his or her ability to live by basic Christian principles.

What do you think enables this person to live by Christian principles? Check those that apply. He/she:

____ seems clear about where he/she is headed.
____ is able to focus on the important things.
____ says "no" a lot.
____ has lots of money and pays people to help him/her.
____ prays constantly.
____ has read a great how-to book and followed it step by step.
____ has a supportive community of faith.
____ other.

- What qualities do you admire about his or her life?

- Share a story about this person that demonstrates his or her ability to live by Christian principles.

- As a group, compile a list of some of the common threads in these stories. What qualities do these people share?

Discuss as a group.

> ### Consider this
>
> "In the end, everyone is our teacher, on one level or another. The child is our teacher, our friends, our family, the stranger on the street. Every experience is a challenge; a teaching is always hidden in it."
>
> Rabbi David A. Cooper, quoted in
> *Spiritual Literacy: Reading The Sacred in Everyday Life*, 432–433
>
> ■ Share a story about a lesson you learned from an unexpected person or experience.

Read aloud and discuss

Joseph and his brothers

We can turn to the Scriptures to find examples of people living by their principles. Certainly, not all biblical characters lived ideal lives. Like us, they struggled to choose wisely and sometimes failed. The story of Joseph and his brothers is a good example.

Joseph's brothers, jealous of the favor that their father showered upon Joseph, sold him into slavery. Joseph's gift as an interpreter of dreams allowed him to advise Pharaoh about an upcoming famine in time for the country of Egypt to prepare for it. As a result of Joseph's wise and helpful use of his gift, Pharaoh gave him a position of power in his household. Meanwhile, Joseph's family suffered because of the famine. In desperation, the brothers traveled to Egypt to ask for food, unaware that Joseph, their brother, was alive.

Genesis 45:4-11a

4 Then Joseph said to his brothers, "Come closer to me." And they came closer. He said, "I am your brother, Joseph, whom you sold into Egypt. 5 And now do not be distressed, or angry with yourselves, because you sold me here; for God sent me before you to preserve life. 6 For the famine has been in the land these two years; and there are five more years in which there will be neither plowing nor harvest. 7 God sent me before you to preserve for you a remnant on earth, and to keep alive for you many survivors. 8 So it was not you who sent me here, but God; he has made me a father to Pharaoh, and lord of all his house

and ruler over all the land of Egypt. **⁹ Hurry and go up to my father and say to him, 'Thus says your son Joseph, God has made me lord of all Egypt; come down to me, do not delay. ¹⁰ You shall settle in the land of Goshen, and you shall be near me, you and your children and your children's children, as well as your flocks, your herds, and all that you have. ¹¹ I will provide for you there.**

- How did Joseph choose to respond to his brothers?
- How else might Joseph have responded?
- What do you imagine were the principles that guided Joseph's actions?

A further look

Read and discuss.

We can also learn from those who fail to choose wisely. In the story of the rich ruler, the man earnestly desired to follow Jesus and yet he could not do the one thing Jesus asked of him. Read aloud Luke 18:18-26 and discuss the questions.

- What principle did Jesus ask the rich ruler to live by?
- What made it difficult for the ruler to do what Jesus asked?
- In what ways, if any, can you relate to the rich ruler?
- What lessons about principles and making smart choices do you learn from this story?

Discovery

Read aloud and discuss.

Timara and Winston's story

Six years ago, just before Timara and Winston's first child was born, they resolved to raise their child according to the principles they valued.

"Maybe we were being idealistic," laughs Timara, "but we had hoped to eat together as a family every night, use only cloth diapers, limit television viewing, and attend church every week."

"We started out doing well," recalls Winston, "but then the washing machine broke down and my work schedule changed. Before we knew it we'd bought disposable diapers and abandoned a few of our other goals."

Today, Timara and Winston are the parents of three children under the age of six. They attend church most Sundays. Although weekdays tend to be chaotic, they manage to eat their weekend meals together.

"On the evenings when I work," says Timara, "I end up plopping the kids in front of the television with a microwave dinner so I have time to get ready. I don't feel good about this, but I also don't see many other choices."

Winston adds, "But we never watch TV on Friday night. Friday night is family night. We eat together and then play games and talk."

- Given Timara and Winston's ideas and choices, what do you think are some of the principles they value?
- What are some of the challenges they face?
- What advice would you give them?
- Though your life situation may be different, to what aspects of Timara and Winston's life can you relate?

Discuss as a group.

Consider this

- Thinking of your life as a road to be traveled, which of these two routes do you take most often—the country road or the freeway? Why?

Read aloud.

Actions and principles

As we have seen, our actions reveal what we value, and the people, activities, and choices we value provide a helpful clue to discerning our guiding principles. In the following exercise, you will look at your own life and consider what your actions say about your principles.

Provide paper and pens. Read questions aloud and allow time for group members to complete the activity.

Step 1: List five major events in your life. (Some examples might be starting your first job, getting married, or moving to a new city).

Step 2: Choose an event that you would be comfortable discussing with group members and list some of the choices you made during that time in your life. (For example, moving to a new city might have involved both choosing to live closer to family and choosing to leave a secure job.)

Step 3: In groups of two, share the event you selected and some of the choices you made. Then, consider these questions with your partner.

- What factors and relationships influenced your decisions? (For example, you might say that your choice was influenced by your family and messages you received from your occupation.)

- What do the choices you made reveal about what you valued at the time? (For example, a choice to move might reveal that you valued living in a certain setting or being closer to family.)

- As you reflect on the experience, what principles emerge as being important to you at that time?

A further look

Read aloud and discuss the question.

In this chapter you have considered the principles that have guided your life, especially during moments of decision. As Christians we believe that God is with us, supporting and guiding us, in the midst of any decision we make. Isaiah writes, "The LORD will guide you continually, and satisfy your needs in parched places, and make your bones strong" (Isaiah 58:11a).

- Share a story of a moment in your life when you felt that God was guiding you. What happened? How did you feel God's presence?

Romans 8:28

28 We know that all things work together for good for those who love God, who are called according to his purpose.

- How have you seen "things work together for good" in the midst of choices that you or others have made?

Wrap-up

Before you go, take time for the following:

- Group ministry task

- Review

- Personal concerns and prayer concerns

- Closing prayers

Daily walk

Bible readings

Day 1
Isaiah 12:2-6

Day 2
Isaiah 35:1-7

Day 3
Isaiah 40:3-8

Day 4
Isaiah 40:28-31

Day 5
Isaiah 55:1-9

Day 6
Isaiah 58:11-12

Day 7
Isaiah 60:19-20

Verse for the journey

"Set up road markers for yourself, make yourself guideposts; consider well the highway, the road by which you went" (Jeremiah 31:21a).

Thought for the journey

Continue taking time to consider some of the major choices you have made in your life. What principles have guided you? How have you experienced God's presence in the midst of these moments of decision?

Prayer for the journey

Holy God, source of strength, with gratitude we remember how you have guided us in the past. Accompany us as we travel forward. Amen

3 From Principles to Mission Statement

Focus

A mission statement can be a helpful tool for Christians who are seeking to make wise choices.

Community building

Allow time for each member of the group to respond.

Option

Tell about the household chore that you are most likely to put off doing. What causes you to procrastinate?

■ Which of the following common New Year's resolutions would be hardest for you to keep and why?
  a. Spend less money.
  b. Go on a diet.
  c. Quit smoking.
  d. Exercise every day.
  e. Watch less television.
  f. Get organized.
  g. Other.

Check-in

■ Share a high point and a low point from your week. When all have shared, pray for each person in the group, saying in unison: "Jesus, our protector, we pray for (*name*). Support him/her in difficult moments and rejoice with him/her in joyful times. Help the rest of us see how we are your hands."

Opening prayer

We thank you, God of all people, for creating each of us with a unique calling to serve you. Amen

Discovery

Group reporting

- Share an insight about yourself that you gained while reflecting on the choices you have made and the principles that have guided you.

Read and discuss.

What is a mission statement?

In the past two chapters you have examined your daily choices and considered the principles that guide your life. A reflection on these issues leads to this question: "Is there an ultimate purpose behind my daily choices?" As Christians we believe that God has a purpose for each of our lives. Unfortunately, we are not born with a statement of purpose attached to us like an owner's manual. Our mission or purpose in life is something that may take time to discover.

A mission statement articulates the principles that we hope will guide our daily choices. It reflects our understanding of God's purpose for our lives. In recent years, many churches, businesses, and other organizations have found it helpful to write mission statements. As these organizations do their daily work, their mission statements help them to make smart, principle-based choices.

- What images does the word "mission" bring to your mind?
- What may be some of the benefits of having a mission statement?
- How do you think a mission statement can guide choices?
- Tell a story about a church or business following a mission statement.

Discuss as a group.

> **Consider this**
>
> A short while before his death [Rabbi Zusya said], "In the world to come I shall not be asked: 'Why were you not Moses?' I shall be asked: 'Why were you not Zusya?'"
>
> <div align="right">Rabbi Zusya, quoted in <i>The Cloister Walk</i> by Kathleen Norris (New York: Riverhead, 1996), 63</div>
>
> ■ What do you think Rabbi Zusya meant by this statement? Do you agree with him? Why or why not?
>
> ■ In what ways are you tempted to compare yourself to others?

Read and discuss

John the Baptist

John the Baptist provides a helpful example of a biblical person who had a clear sense of mission. John was Jesus' cousin. All four Gospels portray John as having a central role in preparing people for Jesus' ministry. He is described as a fiery preacher who lived in the wilderness and drew great crowds as he proclaimed his message. John's message of repentance centered on demanding that his hearers turn from their former ways of life and lead a more godly life. The Greek word for "repent" literally means "to turn around." Some people wondered if John was the Messiah.

John 1:19-27

[19] This is the testimony given by John when the Jews sent priests and Levites from Jerusalem to ask him, "Who are you?" [20] He confessed and did not deny it, but confessed, "I am not the Messiah." [21] And they asked him, "What then? Are you Elijah?" He said, "I am not." "Are you the prophet?" He answered, "No." [22] Then they said to him, "Who are you? Let us have an answer for those who sent us. What do you say about yourself?" [23] He said, "I am the voice of one crying out in the wilderness, 'Make straight the way of the Lord,'" as the prophet Isaiah said.

[24] Now they had been sent from the Pharisees. [25] They asked him, "Why then are you baptizing if you are neither the Messiah, nor Elijah, nor the prophet?" [26] John answered them, "I baptize with water. Among you stands one whom you do not know, [27] the one who is coming after me; I am not worthy to untie the thong of his sandal."

- What does John reveal about who he is and who he is not?
- What is John's mission?
- How do you suppose having a strong sense of mission guided John in his life?
- How do you think our identity (our sense of who we are) is related to our mission (what we are called to do with our lives)?
- How might knowing both who you are and who you are not help you in considering your mission?

A further look

Read aloud and discuss.

A popular bracelet sports the letters "W.W.J.D." The letters refer to the phrase, "What would Jesus do?" Wearers of the bracelet say that the letters "W.W.J.D." serve as a sort of mission statement, a constant reminder to follow Jesus' example as they live their lives. A young person says that the bracelet reminds him that he shouldn't put down other people because of how they dress. A nurse uses the bracelet to remind herself to serve others lovingly, even her crankiest patients.

- Some Christians believe that it might be better to ask the question, "What would Jesus have us do?" What do you think?
- Would a "W.W.J.D." bracelet be a helpful reminder for you as you seek to make smart choices? Why or why not?

Discovery

Read aloud and discuss.

The early church communities: Acts 2:44-47

44 All who believed were together and had all things in common; 45 they would sell their possessions and goods and distribute the proceeds to all, as any had need. 46 Day by day, as they spent much time together in the temple, they broke bread at home and ate their food with glad and generous hearts, 47 praising God and having the goodwill of all the people. And day by day the Lord added to their number those who were being saved.

- This passage describes the early church community. What actions are central to their life together?
- What principles do you see revealed in their actions?
- What mission statement might you write for this early church community to help it keep its principles in mind as they minister together?

Discuss as a group.

Consider this

- What principles are revealed in this picture?
- What might be some elements that this congregation would include in its mission statement?

A further look

Read and discuss.

The Cortez family life has become more chaotic since the two children, Maria and Juan, have become adolescents. Rebekah Cortez says, "I've become the family chauffeur, driving the kids to and from their activities. Sometimes I even eat in the car."

Carlos, Rebekah's husband, who works two jobs, adds, "I love my family. But how do I choose between providing for their physical needs and spending time with them?"

Some people have observed that, like churches and other organizations, families can benefit from having a mission statement.

- How could developing a family mission statement help the Cortez family stay connected?
- Can you think of families that have a strong sense of mission? What are they like? How does this common sense of mission unite them?

Wrap-up

Before you go, take time for the following:

- Group ministry task

- Review

- Personal concerns and prayer concerns

- Closing prayers

Daily walk

Bible readings

Day 1
Isaiah 42:5-9

Day 2
1 Samuel 3:1-10

Day 3
1 Corinthians 12:12-26

Day 4
1 Corinthians 12:27-31

Day 5
1 Corinthians 13:1-8

Day 6
Romans 8:28-39

Day 7
Isaiah 43:1-2

Verse for the journey

"The human mind plans the way, but the LORD directs the steps" (Proverbs 16:9).

Thought for the journey

In preparation for writing your mission statement, consider: Who has God called you to be (and not to be)? To what principles and activities in your life do you wish to give priority?

Prayer for the journey

Jesus, our teacher, as we seek to order our lives, remind us to center ourselves around you. Amen

4 Creating Your Own Mission Statement

Focus

By discerning your gifts and considering the principles by which you want to live you can create a mission statement.

Community building

Complete this exercise as a group. If the characters listed are unfamiliar, choose five of your own.

Option

Provide magazines and newspapers for the group. Look at several advertisements and suggest what each says about the mission of the company represented.

- If the cartoon character Superman had a mission statement it might read: "I will use my extraordinary strength to save the world from evil." For each of the characters below, discuss what you think his or her mission statement might be. Do as many as time allows.
    a. Santa Claus
    b. Oscar the Grouch from *Sesame Street*
    c. Romeo and Juliet
    d. Robin Hood
    e. Winnie the Pooh
    f. Dorothy from *The Wizard of Oz*
    g. Ebenezer Scrooge

Check-in

- Share a high point and a low point from your week. When all have shared, pray for each person in the group, saying in unison: "God, you know us better than we know ourselves. Grant to (*name*) what she/he needs most in her/his life."

Opening prayer

God, source of all our blessings, give us the wisdom to discern your purpose for our lives and the courage to live as your gifted people. Amen

Discovery

Group reporting

- Share an insight you gained while reflecting on some of the activities and principles that you wish to give priority in your life.

Read aloud and discuss.

Gifts and talents

As we consider our personal mission, it is helpful to think about our identity, or who God has called us to be. Each of us has been created as a unique individual with particular gifts and talents. Our mission grows out of both who we are and the principles we hold.

In this passage, the apostle Paul discusses the uniqueness of each individual's gifts. He reminds the Christians that though they each have a unique calling, their gifts contribute to the ministry of the whole community.

Romans 12:4-8

4 For as in one body we have many members, and not all the members have the same function, 5 so we, who are many, are one body in Christ, and individually we are members one of another. 6 We have gifts that differ according to the grace given to us: prophecy, in proportion to faith; 7 ministry, in ministering; the teacher, in teaching; 8 the exhorter, in exhortation; the giver, in generosity; the leader, in diligence; the compassionate, in cheerfulness.

- How have you seen the gifts Paul mentions put into action in your life and the lives of others?
- How have you seen Christians use their gifts to support one another and work together?
- Name other gifts, besides the ones Paul mentions in this passage, that are present in the Christian community.

Provide paper and pens for the exercise.

Now take some time to consider your own gifts.

Step 1: Write down 10 of your gifts and talents.

Step 2: Choose one of your gifts and talents that you use frequently and circle it.

Step 3: Choose one of your gifts and talents that you rarely use and draw a box around it.

Step 4: In pairs, discuss these questions:
- How have you made good use of the circled gift?
- What has prevented you from using the boxed gift?

Discuss together.

Consider this

- How are the members of the body of Christ like puzzle pieces?

A further look

Read Bible texts and discuss as a group.

- What do these passages tell you about the mission of the Christian church?

    Matthew 28:19
    Matthew 25:31-40
    Mark 12:28-31
    Matthew 10:7-8

Discovery

Read aloud and consider the questions together.

Constraints and demands

When we look at a list of principles, it may be difficult to decide which ones to focus on when forming our own mission statement. Each principle has value. But we are finite human beings. We operate with very real constraints and demands. Our personal mission needs to consider both our principles and the reality of daily life.

Many have made the point that whether or not we make conscious choices, we are always saying "yes" to one thing and "no" to something else. Often we must choose between two things we value. For example, choosing to spend more time at work may mean choosing not to spend time with family or friends.

- What are some of the constraints or demands in your life?

- Share an example from your own life that shows a time when your choice to say "yes" to one thing meant you had to say "no" to something else.

- On a scale of 1 to 10 (10 being the most difficult), how difficult do you find:
    a. setting priorities?
    b. saying "no" to people?
    c. focusing on one task at a time?
    d. choosing between two things that you value highly?

Discuss as a group.

Consider this

We all are one in mission; we all are one in call,
our varied gifts united by Christ, the Lord of all.
A single great commission compels us from above
to plan and work together that all may know Christ's love.

We all are called to service, to witness in God's name.
Our ministries are diff'rent; our purpose is the same:
to touch the lives of others with God's surprising grace,
so ev'ry folk and nation may feel God's warm embrace."

From "We All Are One in Mission" *With One Voice* 755, v. 1–2 (Minneapolis: Augsburg Fortress, 1995). Text by Rusty Edwards. Text copyright © 1986 Hope Publishing Co. All rights reserved. Used by permission.

- How can creating a mission statement help you "to touch the lives of others with God's surprising grace"?

Read aloud and discuss.

Guidelines for composing a mission statement

The first thing to remember when putting together your mission statement is to keep it simple—no longer than one or two sentences. If you make your mission statement clear and concise it will be of more practical help to you.

Second, remember that your mission statement is unique to you and connected to the overall mission of other Christians.

Third, as you live out your mission, know that it will affect your relationships with everyone, including God. You may want to consider how putting your mission statement into practice will affect others in your life.

Fourth, make sure that the goals articulated in your mission statement are within your power to accomplish. They should center on your own actions rather than the responses of others.

Finally, your mission statement can (and should) be evaluated and revised at any point in the future. As you work today consider your present situation.

- What do you find most exciting about writing a mission statement? Most challenging?

Read together. Instruct group members to write their mission statements between sessions.

- To write your mission statement begin by choosing three key principles upon which you want to center your life. Then choose three of the gifts with which God has blessed you. In choosing these principles and gifts consider your current life circumstances and constraints. Ask yourself: Which principles and gifts can best help you to carry out your mission at this time?

Read and discuss.

Samantha's mission statement

Samantha is a single woman in her mid-20s. She works as a mail carrier. She listed as her three principles: care for God's creation, compassion for others, and gratitude. She listed as her three gifts: patience, friendliness, and the ability to listen well. Samantha wrote the following mission statement: "My mission is to take the time to appreciate what is beautiful in other people and the world around me, and in my words and actions confess that everyone and everything is part of God's creation."

- How did Samantha incorporate her gifts and principles into her mission statement?
- How does Samantha's mission statement relate to a broader Christian mission?

A further look

Discuss together.

"The place God calls you to is the place where your deep gladness and the world's deep hunger meet."

From Frederick Buechner, *Wishful Thinking: A Theological ABC*, (New York: HarperCollins, 1973) 73

- What brings you "deep gladness"?
- For what do you think the world is hungering?

Wrap-up

Before you go, take time for the following:

- Group ministry task

- Review

- Personal concerns and prayer concerns

- Closing prayers

Daily walk

Bible readings

Day 1
Matthew 7:7-11

Day 2
Mark 4:35-41

Day 3
Luke 1:26-38

Day 4
Luke 2:8-20

Day 5
John 14:27

Day 6
Hebrews 11:1-3, 8-12

Day 7
Philippians 4:10-13

Verse for the journey

[Jesus said] "You did not choose me but I chose you. And I appointed you to go and bear fruit, fruit that will last, so that the Father will give you whatever you ask him in my name" (John 15:16).

Thought for the journey

Write down your three key principles, your three key gifts, and your mission statement (remember, it doesn't have to be perfect!).

Prayer for the journey

All-seeing God, awaken in us a vision for your mission in our lives and give us the ability to mold what we see into words and actions. Amen

5 Christian Principles into Practice

Focus

As you put your mission statement into practice you need to consider how your Christian principles influence your roles and relationships.

Community building

Allow time for each member of the group to respond.

- Consider some of the roles that are important in your life. These roles might include parent, spouse, employee, student, church member, and consumer. Share one of your first memories or experiences in one of these roles (for example, your first memory as a parent or your first day on the job).

Check-in

- Share a high point and a low point from your week. When all have shared, pray for the person on your right, saying: "God of power, strengthen (*name*) as she/he seeks to serve you."

Option

In pairs, play a game "20 questions," in which the first person thinks about one of his or her roles and the second person tries to guess what it is. Questions might include: How long have you been in this role? Do you earn money in this role? Is this role gender-based? When each person in the pair has had a turn, share your roles with the larger group.

Opening prayer

God of new beginnings, each day we face a multitude of tasks and challenges. Surround us with your wise guidance. Amen

Discovery

Group reporting

- Those who wish may share their mission statements with the group.

Read and discuss.

Words and actions

The writer of 1 John wrote: "Little children, let us love, not in word or speech, but in truth and action" (1 John 3:18).

- What is the difference between loving in "word or speech" and loving in "truth and action"?
- Share a story about a time when you experienced love through the action of another.

Read aloud.

Relationships and roles

A mission statement is a concise summary of how we want to live. The next step is to put your mission statement into action in the daily choices you make. As you begin to put your mission statement into practice it will be helpful to consider how it will affect some of the many relationships and roles that are central in your life.

For example, in the last session we learned that Samantha's mission statement was "to take the time to appreciate what is beautiful in other people and the world around me, and in my words and actions confess that everyone and everything is part of God's creation." As she seeks to put her mission statement into practice, Samantha considers some of the various relationships and roles that are a part of her daily life. Her list of relationships includes: God, self, parents, friends, and sister. She lists "mail carrier, caretaker of God's creation, consumer, neighbor, and citizen" as some of her primary roles.

Divide group into pairs to complete the exercise.

In pairs, brainstorm some of the relationships and roles that are most important in your life. Use your partner as a resource to help you. Create a list.

Choose three roles or relationships from your list. For each of these write a statement that indicates how you would like your mission statement to impact these relationships or roles.

For example, Samantha chose her relationship with her sister and wrote, "I plan to give her a phone call at least once a week and tell her how much I appreciate her." She chose her role as a mail carrier and wrote, "I will try my best to greet everyone on my route with kindness."

You may want to complete statements for the rest of your roles and relationships between sessions.

Discuss with the larger group.

- As a group, share some of the ways you see your mission statement impacting your daily roles and relationships.

Discuss together.

Consider this

- Tell about a time when you needed to juggle a variety of roles and responsibilities. What was the experience like for you? What did you learn about yourself through this experience?

A further look

Have someone read these passages aloud. Discuss as a group.

Read Isaiah 6:8 and Jeremiah 1:4-8. In these passages, God calls to Isaiah and Jeremiah and sends them on a mission.

- How do Jeremiah and Isaiah differ in the way they respond to God's call?
- As you consider God's mission for your life, do you find yourself responding more like Isaiah or Jeremiah?
- In what ways are you like Isaiah?
- In what ways are you like Jeremiah?
- What might prevent you from fulfilling your mission?

41

Discovery

Read and discuss.

Finding support

As we put our mission statement into practice, seeking to make smart choices in our daily life, we need the support of other Christians. The scriptures continually remind us of the role of friendship and the religious community in the lives of believers. Even Jesus was blessed by the support and care of others during his earthly ministry (see Luke 19:1-6 and John 12:1-8).

In the following passage the writer of the letter to the Hebrews reminds the readers that the Christian community includes people of faith from all times and places.

Hebrews 12:1-2

¹ Therefore, since we are surrounded by so great a cloud of witnesses, let us also lay aside every weight and the sin that clings so closely, and let us run with perseverance the race that is set before us, ² looking to Jesus the pioneer and perfecter of our faith, who for the sake of the joy that was set before him endured the cross, disregarding its shame, and has taken his seat at the right hand of the throne of God.

- Who cheers you on as you "run the race" of life?
- How can "looking to Jesus" help Christians to fulfill their own missions?
- Consult the list of relationships that you made earlier in this chapter. Of the people on that list, who can support you as you seek to live out your mission statement? How can they support you?

Discuss as a group.

Consider this

- How can living out one's Christian mission be compared to running in a marathon?
- Where are you in the race?

Discuss as a group.

Spiritual resources

- Which of the following spiritual resources do you find most helpful and why?
    a. prayer
    b. Bible study
    c. meditation
    d. listening to Christian music
    e. public worship
    f. service to others
    g. retreats
    h. reading devotionals
    i. other

- Which of these resources would you like to use to aid you in living out your mission statement?

A further look

Discuss as a group.

Jesus said, "Whoever is faithful in a very little is faithful also in much" (Luke 16:10a). Ideally, as you put your mission statement into practice you will become more faithful to God in both the small and large aspects of your life. With your mission statement in front of you, answer the following questions.

- How will putting your mission statement into practice affect the way you:
    a. drive a car
    b. spend your spare time
    c. play games
    d. spend your money
    e. relate to strangers

Wrap-up

Before you go, take time for the following:

- Group ministry task

- Review

- Personal concerns and prayer concerns

- Closing prayers

Daily walk

Bible readings

Day 1
Romans 13:8-10

Day 2
Romans 14:19

Day 3
Philippians 2:1-5

Day 4
1 Thessalonians 5:12-18

Day 5
1 Peter 4:7-11

Day 6
John 4:7-12

Day 7
John 13:31-35

Verse for the journey

"Therefore encourage one another and build up each other, as indeed you are doing" (1 Thessalonians 5:11).

Thought for the journey

Seek out a trusted friend or family member and share your mission statement with him or her. If you wish, ask this person for prayers and support.

Prayer for the journey

Jesus our friend, provide us with companions who will support and encourage us as we seek to make wise choices. Amen

6 Smart Choices for a Lifetime

Focus

God continues to renew your commitment to practicing Christian principles through the ongoing support of your faith community.

Community building

Invite group members to respond to the question.

- These are inventions that could be part of the future. Which of these would you be most likely to use and why?
    a. a computer that prepares and serves meals
    b. a device that locates any lost item
    c. a form of transportation that instantaneously takes you to your destination
    d. a machine that keeps your home completely clean with no help needed from you
    e. a perpetually blooming garden
    f. a pill that keeps you eternally young

Option

Share a dream that you would like to fulfill in the next 10 years.

Check-in

- Share a high point and a low point from your week. When all have shared, pray for each person in the group, saying in unison: "God, remind (*name*) that you will guide her/him in the future as you have in the past."

Opening prayer

Jesus our hope, though we do not know what lies ahead, we do know that you are constantly present among us. In all the circumstances of our lives, inspire us to trust in you. Amen

Discovery

Group reporting

- As you have shared your mission statement with family and friends, how have they responded?

- Do you find their responses:
    a. encouraging?
    b. frustrating?
    c. surprising?
    d. predictable?
    e. other?

- Explain.

Read and discuss.

Encountering obstacles

Over the course of this small-group study, you have considered your choices and principles, written a mission statement, and begun to think about how to implement that mission in your life. Now comes the difficult part—making smart choices every day. Even when we are well-intentioned we sometimes encounter obstacles that prevent us from making choices based on our principles.

The following passage recounts events from the night that Jesus was arrested. Immediately prior to his arrest, Jesus predicted that all of his disciples would desert him. In response, Peter said, "Though all become deserters because of you, I will never desert you" (Matthew 26:33). Jesus predicted that Peter would deny him. Peter pledged his loyalty, saying, "Even though I must die with you, I will not deny you" (Matthew 26:35).

Matthew 26:69-75

69 Now Peter was sitting outside in the courtyard. A servant-girl came to him and said, "You also were with Jesus the Galilean." 70 But he denied it before all of them, saying, "I do not know what you are talking about." 71 When he went out to the porch, another servant-girl saw him, and she said to the bystanders, "This man was with Jesus of Nazareth." 72 Again he denied it with an oath, "I do not know the man." 73 After a little while the bystanders came up and said to Peter, "Certainly you are also one of them, for your accent betrays you." 74 Then he began to curse, and he swore an oath, "I do not know the man!" At that moment the cock crowed. 75 Then Peter remembered what Jesus had said: "Before the cock crows, you will deny me three times." And he went out and wept bitterly.

- When Peter vowed that he would not desert Jesus, he was proclaiming that he would live by the principle of faithfulness. What obstacles did Peter encounter in trying to remain faithful to Jesus?

- What resources might have helped Peter to choose wisely in this situation?

- What are some of the obstacles that may prevent you from living by your principles and making smart choices every day?

- Despite Peter's denial of Jesus, he went on to become one of the foremost leaders in the early Christian church. How might knowing this encourage you in those moments when you fail to live by your principles?

Discuss as a group.

Consider this

- When are some of the times in life that obstacles or inconveniences can be beneficial? You may wish to share a story from your own experience.

A further look

Read text and discuss questions.

Read Micah 7:7-8.

- What do you think the prophet means when he writes, "When I fall, I shall rise"?

- How might this passage serve as an inspiration to you when you fail to make smart choices?

Discovery

Read aloud and discuss.

Patience

A mission statement can help you to make significant changes in your life. However, change takes time. No matter how hard you work at putting your mission statement into practice, positive results may not be immediately apparent. The following verse from the letter of James was written to encourage first-century Christians as they awaited Jesus' return. The writer's advice is helpful to Christians who need patience in any situation.

James 5:7

7 Be patient, therefore, beloved, until the coming of the Lord. The farmer waits for the precious crop from the earth, being patient with it until it receives the early and late rains.

- What lesson can you learn from the image of a farmer waiting for crops to grow?

- On a scale of 1 to 10 (1: I can't even wait for the green light at traffic signals; 10: I could sit around and watch corn grow), how patient are you?

- In what ways will you need to be patient as you seek to fulfill your mission statement?

Discuss as a group.

> **Consider this**
>
> "When we become Christians, as children or as adults, we are not simply converted all at once. We begin on the path of spiritual life, but there are many areas of our lives still to be claimed by God. Spiritual growth is the process by which this happens."
>
> From *How to Keep a Spiritual Journal* by Ron Klug, (Minneapolis: Augsburg, 1982) 13
>
> ■ How has the process of writing a mission statement helped you to grow spiritually?
>
> ■ What areas of your life still need "to be claimed by God"?

Read aloud.

Covenant groups

In chapter 5, you considered resources to help you fulfill your mission statement. One of the most important of these resources is the community of faith. In Paul's letter to the Romans he writes, "For I am longing to see you so that I may share with you some spiritual gift to strengthen you—or rather so that we may be mutually encouraged by each other's faith, both yours and mine" (Romans 1:11-12).

Paul understood that Christian community provides believers with an opportunity both to give and receive spiritual support. Community comes in many forms including worship, small groups, and committee work.

Christians can benefit especially from one-to-one spiritual support. In the Old Testament David and Jonathan made a covenant of friendship with each other. This covenant led Jonathan to protect David when he was in danger (1 Samuel 18:1-5).

You can give and receive help in fulfilling your mission statements by forming groups of two or three and making a covenant of support for one another. This will help to hold you accountable and give you needed encouragement as you face the challenge of choosing wisely every day. Some ways in which you might offer your support to each other include making weekly phone calls, meeting together on a regular basis, praying for each other, and writing each other notes of encouragement.

Discuss covenant options.

As a group, decide whether you want to participate in covenant groups, and if so, for how long. Then divide into groups of two or three. Allow time for each group to agree on a covenant.

Another option is continuing to meet periodically as a whole group. If you choose this option, you will also benefit from writing a group covenant.

Read aloud and discuss.

Reviewing your mission statement

You did not write your mission statement in stone, and for good reason. Mission statements are meant to be flexible. As we journey through life, God calls us to minister in various ways and situations. Our roles and relationships are always changing. For this reason, we need to review and revise our mission statements periodically.

Here are some questions you might want to ask yourself when trying to decide if it is time to change your mission statement:

- Have my life circumstances changed since I wrote or last revised my mission statement?
- Is my mission statement making an ongoing positive difference in my life?
- Is God calling me in a new direction in my life?

A further look

Read aloud and discuss.

Hopefully, your participation in this small group has inspired you to make a lifetime of wise choices. Of course, the real work of putting your mission statement into practice happens as you make decisions, both large and small, every day. Making smart choices is a daily discipline that happens in your home, at your workplace, on the highway, or at the grocery store. These ordinary acts reflect the principles we value and serve as a witness of our faith to others.

- Return to the image of your ideal life that you were asked to consider in "Thought for the Journey," chapter 1 (page 18). In what ways has your participation in this group helped to bring you closer to that image?
- In what other ways have you benefited from participating in this group?
- What are some of your hopes and fears as you seek to make smart choices every day?

Wrap-up

Before you go, take time for the following:

- Group ministry task

- Review

- Personal concerns and prayer concerns

- Closing prayers

Daily walk

Bible readings

Day 1
Psalm 16

Day 2
Psalm 33

Day 3
Psalm 61:1-5

Day 4
Psalm 63:1-8

Day 5
Psalm 91

Day 6
Psalm 121

Day 7
Psalm 146

Verse for the journey

"May you be made strong with all the strength that comes from his glorious power, and may you be prepared to endure everything with patience, while joyfully giving thanks to the Father" (Colossians 1:11-12a).

Thought for the journey

Think about your life as it extends into the future. As you anticipate major events ahead, how do you imagine your mission statement will influence you as you navigate through them?

Prayer for the journey

God of our future, support us, strengthen us, and guide us each moment of every day so that we may make choices with wisdom and love. Amen

Appendix

Group directory

Record information about group members here.

Names	Addresses	Phone numbers

Group commitments

"Do not be conformed to this world, but be transformed by the renewing of your minds, so that you may discern what is the will of God—what is good and acceptable and perfect" (Romans 12:2).

- For our time together, we have made the following commitments to each other

- Goals for our study of this topic are

- Our group ministry task is

- My personal action plan is

Prayer requests

_____

_____

_____

_____

_____

_____

_____

Prayers

■ Closing Prayer

Lord God, you have called your servants to ventures of which we cannot see the ending, by paths as yet untrodden, through perils unknown. Give us faith to go out with good courage, not knowing where we go, but only that your hand is leading us and your love supporting us; through Jesus Christ our Lord. Amen

From *LBW* (page 153) copyright © 1978.

■ The Lord's Prayer

(If you plan to use the Lord's Prayer, record the version your group uses in the next column.)

Resources

Bolles, Richard Nelson. *What Color Is Your Parachute?* Berkeley: Ten Speed Press, 1996.

Brussat, Frederic and Mary Ann. *Spiritual Literacy: Reading The Sacred In Everyday Life.* New York: Scribner, 1996.

Chittister, Joan. *There Is A Season.* Maryknoll, N.Y.: Orbis Books, 1995.

Covey, Stephen R. *The Seven Habits of Highly Effective People.* New York: Simon and Schuster, 1989.

DeGrote-Sorenson, Barbara, and David Allen Sorenson. *'Tis A Gift To Be Simple.* Minneapolis: Augsburg, 1992.

DeGrote-Sorenson, Barbara, and David Allen Sorenson. *Six Weeks to a Simpler Lifestyle.* Minneapolis: Augsburg, 1994.

Hardin, Paula Payne. *What Are You Doing With The Rest Of Your Life? Choices in Midlife.* San Rafael, Calif.: New World Library, 1992.

Luhrs, Janet. *The Simple Living Guide.* New York: Broadway Books, 1997.

Please check the INTERSECTIONS book you are evaluating.

- ☐ The Bible and Life
- ☐ Captive and Free
- ☐ Caring and Community
- ☐ Death and Grief
- ☐ Divorce
- ☐ Faith
- ☐ Following Jesus
- ☐ Jesus: Divine and Human
- ☐ Men and Women
- ☐ Peace
- ☐ Praying
- ☐ Self-Esteem
- ☐ Smart Choices

Please tell us about your small group.

1. Our group had an average attendance of _____.

2. Our group was made up of
   ____ Young adults (19-25 years)
   ____ Adults (most between 25-45 years)
   ____ Adults (most between 45-60 years)
   ____ Adults (most between 60-75 years)
   ____ Adults (most 75 and over)
   ____ Adults (wide mix of ages)
   ____ Men (number) and ____ women (number)

3. Our group (answer as many as apply)
   ____ came together for the sole purpose of studying this INTERSECTIONS book.
   ____ has decided to study another INTERSECTIONS book.
   ____ is an ongoing Sunday school group.
   ____ met at a time other than Sunday morning.
   ____ had only one facilitator for this study.

FOLD CARD IN HERE, SEAL WITH TAPE, AND MAIL TODAY!

Please tell us about your experience with INTERSECTIONS.

4. What I like best about my INTERSECTIONS experience is

5. Three things I want to see the same in future INTERSECTIONS books are

6. Three things I might change in future INTERSECTIONS books are

7. Topics I would like developed for new INTERSECTIONS books are

8. Our group had ____ sessions for the six chapters of this book.

9. Other comments I have about INTERSECTIONS are

Thank you for taking the time to fill out and return this questionnaire.

NO POSTAGE
NECESSARY
IF MAILED
IN THE
UNITED STATES

BUSINESS REPLY MAIL
FIRST-CLASS MAIL   PERMIT NO. 22120   MINNEAPOLIS, MN

POSTAGE WILL BE PAID BY ADDRESSEE

Augsburg Fortress
ATTN INTERSECTIONS TEAM
PO BOX 1209
MINNEAPOLIS MN 55440-8807